KEY TO COUNTY BOUNDARIES

England in Cameracolour
Devon & Cornwall

England in Cameracolour
Devon & Cornwall

Photographs by F. A. H. BLOEMENDAL

Text by ALAN HOLLINGSWORTH

LONDON

IAN ALLAN LTD

First published 1982

ISBN 0 7110 1223 7

© Ian Allan Ltd 1982

Published by Ian Allan Ltd, Shepperton, Surrey;
and printed in Italy by
Graphische Betriebe Athesia, Bolzano

Introduction

The landscape of England's south-west peninsula epitomises the eternal struggle between the immense force of the sea and the massive endurance of ancient rock. For nowhere in this sea-girt promontory is the sea more than twenty miles away and its influence, hard and direct, soft and subtle is everywhere to be felt. The sea has hammered out the shape of Cornwall's granite cape, its restless fingers have slipped into the river valleys of the Camel, the Fal, the Tamar and the Dart and transformed them totally. Although its gales and storms have sculptured the wild rocks of Dartmoor and added to the moor's bleakness and desolation, the ocean's soft warm rains make the lush Devon valleys where the grass grows ten months of the year.

The coast of Devon and Cornwall is England's 'Atlantic Coast' and the water that washes it is oceanic in origin which means that it is part of the vast circulation of warm clear water that swirls northwards from the Caribbean to become first the Gulf Stream and later the North Atlantic Drift. This same stream is also the source of the steady march of storms and depressions across the North Atlantic as the water warmed air mixes with the colder air from northern latitudes. The effect upon Devon and Cornwall is manifold. Not only does the sea itself exert its tempering effect upon the climate, warming the winters and cooling the summers, the moisture laden westerlies add to the effect. Atlantic mildness also means Atlantic wetness and Devon and Cornwall have an annual rainfall half as much again as the English national average. Their coasts also have a high incidence of persistent sea fog (see page 32) — a factor more often responsible for shipwrecks than the traditional wrecker with his lantern. And Atlantic depressions also mean gales and strong winds — the Lizard, for example, experiences up to 30 days of gale force wind in an average year and many times that number of days when the wind is above Force 6 (25-30mph). Such winds mean rough seas and the steady battering of the waves upon the coastline. Although all waves contribute to the steady erosion of the land by the sea, the great pile-drivers which shape the Atlantic coast are the massive waves of the deep ocean, the huge heaves of water seamen call 'swell'. Travelling in trains of waves, the power of this trans-oceanic swell is largely due to the depth of the water and the 'fetch' — the distance over which the creating wind has been blowing. From Cape Cornwall the fetch across the Atlantic deeps is well over 2,000 miles which goes to explain on one level why the peninsula is the shape it is and on another, why surfing is one of the region's attractions.

Whether it be attacking some great headland like Cornwall and Devon or a stony spit sticking out from some tiny beach, the eroding action of the sea follows a regular pattern and the shape of the peninsula itself results from that pattern. The sea pounds against any surface across its path with sand, stones and immense water pressure — a 25ft wave is said to exert 230 horsepower *per foot* length of coast — which widens flaws in the rock, and even granite has flaws. A section of the cliff — or sea wall — collapses, often having been undermined by caves or cavities first. It falls into the sea and is swept away. In time a small bay is created with two headlands — Cornwall abounds in examples. When this happens, the incoming seas are deflected round the headland and come into the coast again some way back from the point. This process gives so many headlands, great and small, a characteristic snake's head shape — on the grand scale look at Cape Cornwall with St Ives' and Mount's Bays behind it or on a grander scale still, look at Lyme Bay and Bridgwater Bay. As the erosion process continues, the sea breaks through behind the headland, makes it an island and, one day, collapses it in turn. We have examples in the Scillies on the grand scale and Kynance Cove (page 54) Godrevy Island (page 40) St Michael's Mount (page 50) on a lesser. In contrast to continuous erosion, bays between headlands tend to fill up with rocks and sand from eroded headlands which form a beach and this protects the shoreline at least until the whole coast is straightened out and the whole process begins again — as in Widemouth Bay (page 26).

The reason why these processes are so slow in the south-west peninsula despite the immense power of the ocean, is the nature of the rocks of which Cornwall and Devon have been hewn. The backbone of the region is granite, an igneous rock which in some early eruption of the Earth's crust flowed upwards from the molten core to disturb and distort still further the already convoluted layers of sedimentary rock left behind by a succession of primordial seas. The heat and pressure of the granite altered the nature of these rocks — sandstone became quartzite, shale turned into slate, limestone into marble. At the same time vapours and liquids rising from the granite cooled to form deposits of minerals — tin, copper, lead, gold and, surprisingly perhaps, the soft white china clay of the St Austell area. But even the heat hardened sedimentary rock (the Cornish generic name is 'kilas') was not as hard as the obtruding granite and it slowly weathered to leave the granite exposed in five great granite vertebrae which form the backbone of Devon and Cornwall — the Land's End peninsula, Carnmenellis near Redruth, Hensbarrow above St Austell, Bodmin Moor and Dartmoor. Even in Cornwall, however, the most prevalent rock is not granite but 'kilas'. Land's End is the only headland composed of granite (page 46) but both the Scilly Islands and St Michael's Mount (page 50) are also made of it. The Lizard is formed from another igneous rock — a schist (ie layered) variety called serpentine (but this is not the reason for the headland's name!) which is a particularly rare and beautifully marked rock. There are also many other distinctive and colourful igneous rocks found in Cornwall — elvan which is harder than granite, catacleuse which takes its name from Cataclew point near Padstow and polyphant, a greyish blue stone spotted with red which was used in Truro Cathedral. 'Kilas' is much duller stuff but comes in a variety of types depending upon the nature of the original rock and the extent to which it has been 'cooked' and altered by the upheaving of the granite. The result is that from Lynton (page 16) with its spectacular sandstone cliffs round to Sidmouth (page 108) and beyond are cliffs of red, grey, black and silver which are the legacy at least in part of what the geologists call appropriately the Devonian period. East of the Exe, the coast of east Devon is made of softer rock than the iron bound cliffs of West Devon and Cornwall which goes to explain how the sea made its deep inroad in carving out Lyme Bay.

As befits a county of rocks, Cornwall is essentially a county of stone buildings. Unlike the rest of the country Cornwall with its thin soils never enjoyed the benefits of massive forests of oak and other timber suitable for building and in consequence timber-framed buildings are virtually non-existent west of the Tamar. Instead, the Cornishman in earlier times had his granite 'moorstones' — blocks of stone lying about on the surface of hills and moors and beaches — which quarrymen call 'presents'. Granite was not quarried until the 17th century and in earlier non-industrial times the task of cutting the immensely hard stone was beyond most builders' resources. Older granite buildings — perhaps even beginning with the prehistoric buildings called 'qoits' — are made of stones of all sizes ranging from huge boulders making up almost one side of the house to roughly dressed corner stones to smaller boulders arranged in uneven courses usually known as random rubble. By the 19th century, however, granite quarrying had become a major industry in Cornwall and blocks could be cut to a required size and laid properly in even courses with fine joints. Cornish granite of this period found a ready market outside the county and among other buildings, Eddystone lighthouse and Tower Bridge were made from it.

The Cornishmen also had slate. Coming from the ever-present 'kilas', slate was easier to work than granite and 'presented' itself below every cliff and rock face in a variety of shapes and sizes. It is a useful walling material and could be used alongside granite. Above all, slate provided an excellent roofing material — compact and strong, non-porous, impervious to frost and light in weight. It too found its way all over the south of England from about the 12th century onwards.

In Cornwall itself therefore, the nature of the typical Cornish building is already apparent — granite rubble walls, slate roof. If we add a few more details — a simple rectangular plan, smallish square windows usually with sashes, occasional slate-hung walls sometimes patterned, slate roofs often covering outshoots nearly down to the ground, slurried with cement to keep off the gales, usually gable ended with few valleys, broad squat chimneys at either end of the building, and a prevalence of porches — some of them of wrought ironwork and brightly coloured glass — we have the essentials of Cornish vernacular architecture reflected in these pages.

If traditional Cornish building materials are granite and slate, those of Devon are 'cob' and thatch — there are also some cob buildings in Cornwall (the local name is 'clob'). Although Devon had supplies of stone for building, notably the granite 'moorstone' of Dartmoor and the cretaceous limestone of the south-east corner, and also enjoyed adequate stands of oak and elm, there is no major tradition of stone-built or timber-framed houses at least partly because of the addiction to cob. The basic material of cob — surely the most traditional of all mankind's building materials — is clay of which Devon has an abundance. The clay was mixed with small stones, straw, water and, quite often, cow dung and cow hair as a binder. The whole mass was then trodden into a malleable mixture usually by human feet. This mix was then laid in layers upon a stone plinth — the cob's shoes — and tramped down in two feet layers. Walls varied in thickness from about 2ft 6in to four feet and each layer took about a week to dry. Corners were rounded and door and window frames were cut to size after the mixture had hardened. Timbers were then fitted and the building was roofed over with thatch thus completing the essential process required by cob construction if it is to last — top and bottom must be kept dry or as they put it in Devon, 'cob needs a good hat and a good pair of shoes.'

Cob buildings, especially farm buildings and walls, were sometimes left in a natural state and in the colour of the basic clay — red in the sandstone areas, buff in the central area of west Devon known as the culm measures. Mostly, however, cob buildings are plastered and white or colour washed — usually cream, buff or pale pink. Plinths are tarred or painted black. Another characteristic of Devon houses is that there is frequent use of side chimneys usually built of brick or stone ascending in a series of sloping shoulders to the eaves with a tall thin stack above that. In North Devon the front door is alongside the chimney stack. Quite often too the top of the chimney has a slate lid supported on corner bricks. Broadhembury (page 8) shows most of these characteristics as does one of the oldest cob houses in Britain — Hayes Barton Manor (page 104). Thatch is as old as cob and the ideal roofing material for it. It is relatively light and does not require massive rafters and purlins. Being based on the use of bundles of reeds or straw it requires a steep pitch — not less than about 50 degrees but it can be swept around angles and allows valleys and dormers and half hips virtually to flow over the entire roof of a building in a soft embrace. In Devon the more usual material is combed wheat reed known as Devon reed which is still in use although Wiltshire long straw and Norfolk reed — a water reed — are also used. In this regard, however, Devon thatch tends to be less opulent that that of some other counties with thinner eaves and shallower hips.

None of this is to suggest that either Cornwall or Devon have no buildings of merit other than those described as traditional. There are notable brick houses in both counties especially in the towns and Exeter and Plymouth; both have superb timber-framed houses — like Mol's Coffee House (page 102). There are also fine stone houses in Devon like the 'longhouses' of Dartmoor and the red sandstone houses of the Torbay area to say nothing of the traditional Cotswold-type houses of the limestone belt in the extreme east of the county.

Traditional vernacular buildings with their roots literally in the soil invariably reflect the nature of their native countryside. Nowhere perhaps is this better seen than in Devon and Cornwall and nowhere, perhaps, is the contrast between adjoining counties so sharply marked — the Tamar is as much an architectural frontier as it is of culture, race and language. The hard rocky weather-beaten face of Cornwall can be seen in its traditional buildings. Except in sheltered coves like Cadgwith or up gentle valleys like the Fal, most houses serve as refuges from the Atlantic blast and their austere rugged style and construction befits their purpose. Granite peninsulas don't easily wash or blow away — nor do granite and slate houses. By contrast, the bulk of Devon is patently much softer. Away from the Atlantic coast and high Dartmoor, the fulsome warmth and richness of the Devon valleys find visual expression in the very cosiness of heavy thatch settling over thick cob. Granite and cob, slate and thatch — they tell the whole story behind Frederick Bloemendal's superb photographs of the face of Devon and Cornwall in the pages that follow.

Salcombe, 1981   *Alan Hollingsworth*

Broadhembury near Honiton, Devon. One of the show villages of Devon, Broadhembury nestles under the slopes of Black Down (929ft) on the edge of the range of hills that begins the great limestone belt that sweeps north-eastwards to the Tees. The houses here are of 'cob' — a mixture of mud, straw, pebbles and dung — a traditional building material in use for centuries. The old Devon saying that cob needs 'a good hat and a pair of shoes' means that the mud walls should be built on a stone plinth and the house should be well thatched. Both are apparent here and the quality of the thatching is due to the care taken of vernacular building by the Devon County Council which has financed a scheme for re-thatching the centre of the village for over 15 years. Devon thatch is thinner with shallower eaves than that of neighbouring counties.

8

Bickleigh Bridge, River Exe, Devon. This ancient sandstone bridge was probably built at the end of the 16th century to replace an earlier wooden one. It carries the A396 from Exeter to Tiverton and also links Bickleigh village on the east bank of the Exe to Bickleigh Castle on the west bank. The Castle was originally the home of Alward, mentioned in Domesday and by the 12th century was a fortified and moated manor owned by the de Bickleigh family. It was further fortified by the Carews in the 15th century and had the honour of being slighted by the Cromwellian general Fairfax. It later fell into further ruin and its buildings were used as barns and farm buildings. Its gatehouse, thatched Norman chapel and the adjoining 17th century farmhouse were restored in recent times and are now open to the public during the summer months.

10

Holcombe Court, Holcombe Rogus, Devon. Once the family home of the Bluetts, Holcombe Court is perhaps the finest Tudor mansion of its kind in Devon. The gatehouse seen here is early Tudor (c1520-30) and is a particularly attractive feature of the house with its tall buttressed tower over the Tudor-arched doorway and the unusual asymmetric stair turret on its left. The windows are original but the large mullioned and transomed windows to the right of the tower date from the end of the 16th century. The fascinating name Rogus comes from a Norman knight whose descendants lived in the village for eight generations.

12

Lynmouth Harbour, Devon. Two Exmoor trout streams, the East Lyn and Hoaroak Water, cascade down from the moor through deep rocky valleys which merge into a magnificent gorge at Watersmeet and run into the sea at Lynmouth, a tiny tidal harbour whose history goes back to before the time of the Armada. But that same history very nearly ended in 1952 when a sudden summer flash storm over the Moor transformed the two gentle chuckling streams into raging red torrents that swept all before them into the sea — bridges, houses, hotels, cars and people. The Lynmouth seen here has been restored and now shows few physical scars of its ordeal. The thatched cottages on the quay have been rebuilt and at the head of the jetty is a replica of General Rawdon's Rhenish-capped beacon tower originally built over a century ago to store salt water for indoor baths.

14

Castle Rock, the Valley of the Rocks, Lynton, Devon. This spectacular dry valley above Lynmouth may well have been created by the Lyn rivers in an earlier geological age when glacial ice blocked their usual outlet to the sea. Certainly Ice Age frost and thousands of years of weathering have carved the local red sandstone into a succession of fantastic shapes. Castle Rock seen here drops over 800ft to the sea and is one of the highest sea cliffs on the British coast.

Watermouth Castle near Combe Martin, Devon. Although it was built on a Norman site, Watermouth Castle dates only from 1825. Baedeker described it in 1906 as a 'large modern castle'. It boasts a banqueting hall, minstrel's gallery, smugglers' tunnel, wine cellars and a museum — and a truly magnificent view across the Bristol Channel.

Ilfracombe, Devon. A view from the cliffs above Hele Bay over the seaward side of Ilfracombe to Lundy on the far horizon. In the left foreground is Blythe's cove and in the centre of the horizon, Bull Point and its lighthouse. Ilfracombe has had a long and distinguished history. Its parish church was begun by the Normans and on Lantern Hill (middle right) is St Nicholas Chapel which since the days of Henry VIII has carried a light to guide local fishermen into the harbour. In earlier times the penitent folk who kept the light burning were afforded 'indulgences'. Nowadays the chapel still carries a leading light and it is presumably the local rate-payers who pay the bill and visiting yachtmen who receive the indulgence. Lundy Island, once an independent domain owing allegiance only to the Crown but now owned by the National Trust — and can be visited — is in fact 24 miles from Ilfracombe. It is three miles long and about a mile wide and is remarkable for the unique flora and fauna its isolation has produced.

20

Clovelly, Devon. Clovelly — a village tumbling down the hill — is mercifully too steep and narrow for the motor car. They use donkeys instead and Clovelly as a result is remarkably unspoiled. Three great names have contributed to its fame and its history. The Carys in the 16th century built a pier and made the tiny place the only safe harbour in the days of square sail between Appledore and Boscastle. The Hamlyns, as Lords of the Manor, preserved the village for decades from would-be exploiters and 'developers' and built the lovely Hobby Drive a mile or so to the east. And Charles Kingsley, who published his immortal *Westward Ho!* in 1855, spent his childhood in the village. His father was rector here from 1830 to 1836 and Kingsley brought Clovelly and the Carys into his story.

Hartland Quay, Devon. Teethmarks of the
Atlantic — the mighty trans-oceanic swell
has bitten deep into the tough carboniferous slate of the north Devon coast
leaving only the hardest ribs of rock uncon-
sumed. This stretch of coastline from Hartland Point southwards is famous for its
mountainous surf and the sport that surf
provides. The great rollers that heave
themselves out of a windless sea have probably had their origins in some great Gulf
Stream storm 2,000 miles and a week
24 away.

Widemouth Bay near Bude, Cornwall. This is Mecca for surfing enthusiasts and it is said that on a good surfing day the pounding of the sea can be heard or felt as much as ten miles away. In this photograph Bude is just visible running along the valley behind the great bluff of Compass Point in the left background. The rocks of Widemouth look like illustrations from a geology textbook — the reefs of sandstone have been cut by the sea as it tears away at the ever-receding cliffs. The contortions of the parallel reefs are the result of the folding of the beds of rock into domes and ridges which have been eroded to leave only the vertical strata behind.

Boscastle, Cornwall. One of the few safe natural harbours on Cornwall's iron-bound north coast, this rocky cliff is none the less a terrifying place for a strange vessel to enter in any but the calmest of weather. Now in the care of the National Trust, Boscastle had its hey-day in the early 19th century, when it was a centre for the export trade in Cornish slate. One feature of interest beyond the outer breakwater is a 'blowhole', which, when wind and tide are right, noisily sends spume and spray high over the harbour entrance.

28

Tintagel, Cornwall. More perhaps by legend than by historical fact, Tintagel Castle, high on the cliff top sheer above the sea, is firmly linked with King Arthur and his saga. Here, it is said, Arthur's parents, Uther Pendragon and Ygraine, first met and fell in love. Tennyson, who wrote of its 'Black cliffs and caves and storms and wind', made the place a Mecca for Victorian tourists inspired by his *Idylls of the King*. Even without the Arthurian saga, however, Tintagel possesses a verifiable romantic history going back more than a thousand years. Originally the site of a Celtic monastery founded by St Julot about AD 400, the foundations of which can still be seen, the castle itself was first built by Earl Richard, a younger brother of King Henry III, in the early part of the 13th century. Subsequently it fell derelict, the sea ate away the isthmus and separated the main wards of the castle — the upper and lower wards on the mainland, the inner ward on the island.

Trevose Head, near Padstow, Cornwall. In the days of sail when Bristol and Falmouth were major transatlantic ports and methods of navigation primitive and uncertain this iron-bound landfall coast was the graveyard of many a fine ship. Quite apart from the high frequency of gales and fierce tides that even a fresh breeze turns into a steep sea, the north Cornish coast is the classic lee shore that all sailors dread and the terror of 'embaying' might well have been invented here when few ships could stand closer than a right angle to the wind. Added to these hazards — and one which despite radar claims victims today — is the sudden descent of blinding sea fog that obliterates all landmarks: there is one in the picture, just offshore. All of this is ample justification for the lighthouse with its powerful light and its penetrating foghorn. It was built in 1847.

Bedruthan Steps, near Newquay, Cornwall. The steps are the large lumps of rock which the sea has torn from the cliffs and legend has it that a local giant Bedruthan used them to step ashore after his morning bathe. The rocks here are crumbling all the time and a celebrated cliff staircase up Pendarves Point overlooking the Steps had to be closed because the cliffs are so unsafe — testimony of the unending power of the sea. The area is one of the many National Trust properties along the Cornish coast.

Newquay, Cornwall. Like so many other places on the coast of Devon and Cornwall, Newquay was a simple fishing village before its discovery as a seaside resort by the Victorians. One of its oldest buildings is 'Huer's House' from which this photograph was taken. It sits on top of the headland overlooking both the harbour and the sea and the huer's job was to watch out for signs of shoals of pilchard in the offing and to call the local fisherman out to catch them by making the appropriate 'hue and cry'. Also called a 'balker' this particular task had an honourable place in many a Cornish fishing village and use of the word goes back to the 16th century.

Carn Brea near Redruth, Cornwall. Old engine houses, stacks and spoil heaps or 'deads' mark the site of a once thriving tin mining industry on Carn Brea just south of Redruth. Carn Brea itself is an offshoot of the granite boss of Carnmenellis — all Cornwall's minerals, including its immensely valuable china clay deposits are found in the granite regions of the county. In the background of the photograph is the crest of Carn Brea — the name means stone hill — with its granite 'tors' and its monument. The monument is to Francis Basset, first Baron de Dunstanville, and enlightened 19th century mineowner who died in 1835 after devoting his life and much of his fortune to improving the working conditions and welfare of the Cornish tin miners.

Godrevy Island and Lighthouse, Cornwall. The Cornish word for the crushed sedimentary rocks which make up much of the county's coastline is 'kilas'. Kilas is, however, subject to many variations in the type and the hardness of the rock itself which explains why in some coastal areas the sea makes indentations at one point but leaves headlands in another. A case in point is Godrevy where the rock is hard sandstone with relatively soft slatey rock to the south in St Ives Bay. Nonetheless the sea is wearing down even the harder rock as the presence of the offshore island demonstrates. Strong tides swirl round these headlands and one victim was a ship containing King Charles I's wardrobe and household effects which was wrecked on the very day he was executed in faraway Whitehall.

St Ives, Cornwall. St Ives is said to have been founded by an Irish missionary St Ia who crossed the Irish Sea in a coracle and built an oratory here in the 5th century. Since then the town has often been host to the rebel and the shiftless from Perkin Warbeck who came from Ireland in 1497, the ill-fated Duke of Monmouth who landed here in 1685 on his way to Sedgemoor, and to the colonies of artists and hippies who add their own peculiar lustre to the little town today. The harbour pier seen here was built by John Smeaton who was the architect of the Eddystone Lighthouse in 1767.

42

Old Engine Houses and Mine Buildings, St Just in Penwith, Cornwall. These ruined engine houses are relics of the last century when Cornwall was the world's largest supplier of copper ore, and as copper mining declined in the face of new sources abroad, for the production of tin. On coastal sites like this one, the mine working extended deep under the sea and the mines were in constant danger of flooding. The demand for adequate pumps led to the development of the Cornish beam engine and its refinement in the hands of Cornish engineers like Richard Trevithick. These simple single-acting non-rotative pumps did sterling work pumping out the mines and many were in service for a century or more. They were housed in buildings like those seen here — the design is found all over the Duchy — tall, gabled, arched-windowed, usually built of coursed granite with the arches and the top of the adjoining chimney stack in red or blue brick.

Land's End, Cornwall. A peninsinula on a peninsula on a peninsula — the land ends but the granite rocks go on, as witness the many lighthouses and the legion of invisible wrecks to emerge again as the Scilly Islands, 28 miles out. They disappear finally into the abyss of the North Atlantic, a few miles further west at the 300 fathom line. Notice how the granite is broken up into rectangular blocks by the fault lines created when the rock was cooling. The action of the sea along this fault line causes the blocks to fall and, over time, for the cliff to crumble and be swept away. Even granite is not impervious to the hydraulic hammer of the waves.

Longships Lighthouse, Land's End, Cornwall. Looking westwards from Land's End across the grotesquely shaped rocks that are said to be remnants of the Arthurian land of Lyonesse which once lay between here and the Scilly Islands 28 miles to the south west. In 1906 even Baedeker was moved to wax lyrical:

'A land of old upheaven from the abyss
By fire, to sink into the abyss again'

In more practical terms, the saw-toothed Longships Ledge is 60ft high in places, is swept by strong tides and has one of the highest incidences of gales and near gales in the Kingdom. This photograph taken on a rare calm day shows clearly the teeth that are usually concealed by spume and spray — with the odd sea fog for good measure.

St Michael's Mount, Cornwall. Called 'Ictis' by the ancients, St Michael's Mount was the legendary home of the giant Cormoran, slain by Jack the Giant Killer. It is a 'miniature' of Mont St Michel in Normandy and its priory, founded by Edward the Confessor, was originally attached to the French house. It had a turbulent history in the Middle Ages, being associated with Perkin Warbeck in 1497 and the Prayer Book Rebellion in 1549. It was extensively and expensively refortified at the outset of the Civil War by its Royalist owner, Sir Arthur Basset. As soon as it came under siege, however, Basset surrendered it to the Parliamentarians, well aware that severe damage to it would, among other things, be the ruin of him. He later sold it to Colonel John Aubyn, an ancestor of Lord St Levan, who still lives there. It was transferred to the National Trust in 1954.

Mullion Cove, Cornwall. Unlike the Land's End peninsula which is entirely granite, the Lizard is made up of a variety of rock types. They are all of igneous origin like granite and as hard and durable as that rock but they are more colourful and varied in texture. The rock at Mullion Cove is greenstone and very hard — it strikes fire with steel like flint — a fine-grained rock which can be used for building. It was used here to build the breakwaters but nonetheless the National Trust who own the harbour face a heavy annual bill for storm damage.

Kynance Cove, Lizard, Cornwall. What gives
Kynance Cove its intense attraction is its
colourful local rock called serpentine. The
unusual colour is dull green with dark markings like those of a serpent's skin and those
markings may be veins or mottling of dark
red or grey. The tall sheer-sided rock on the
left of the headland is Steeple Rock and to
the left again is Asparagus Island with Gull
Rock to the south of it. To see the full glory
of this splendid cove one should visit about
54   three hours before low water.

Cadgwith, Lizard, Cornwall. On the east side of the Lizard peninsula the seas are not so fierce and the rock here is a form of schist — a generic term that covers a group of the oldest rocks found in the country — yet another variety to add to the charm and colour of the Lizard cliffs. Cadgwith itself is a fishing village with attractive thatched cottages around the harbour — and thatch is comparatively rare in Cornwall where 56 slate is the more usual roofing material.

Helford River, Helford, Cornwall. This lovely wooded inlet or 'ria' which comes very close to making Lizard peninsula an island, takes its name from the older name of the river — 'hayle' which is Celtic for a 'salt-river' or estuary. Once used as a port for the export of tin and copper this deep combe has a wealth of tributary creeks and harbours well suited for the clandestine purposes of smugglers and their like. Best known is 'Frenchman's Creek' the setting for Daphne du Maurier's celebrated novel of the same name.

Falmouth, Cornwall. Falmouth owed its early development largely to the efforts of Sir Peter Killigrew who, though a Royalist, persuaded the Commonwealth to grant the right to establish a market on the site. Sir Peter later contributed to the building of the church seen here left of centre — appropriately it is one of few in the United Kingdom devoted to King Charles the Martyr. It has an east window depicting the King holding the headsman's axe. In 1688 Falmouth became a station for the mail packet service and by 1839 it had 39 overseas-mail vessels. The port declined with the coming of the steamship but in 1863 the construction of the railway gave it a new lease of life as a holiday resort.

Carrick Roads, Falmouth, Cornwall. Carrick Roads is the wrist of a hand of the sea which stretches its fingers deep into the wooded Cornish countryside, providing a day-sailing yachtsman with a superb cruising ground of infinite variety. Since the days of Henry VIII it has been guarded by two forts — in the west by Pendennis Castle at Falmouth and in the east by St Mawes Castle, seen in the centre of the photograph. St Mawes Castle, intended as it was for seaward defence, was unprotected on the landward side and fell to Cromwellian troops after only a single day's siege in the Civil War. Pendennis, better sited, lasted for nearly six months.

Lanhydrock, near Bodmin, Cornwall. Built by Royalist Sir Richard Robartes, later Lord Robartes, a tin and wool merchant from Truro, during the Civil War period, Lanhydrock is one of Cornwall's outstanding great houses. It remained in the same family until Lord Clifden, a descendant, gave the property to the National Trust in 1953. A disastrous fire destroyed most of the house in 1881 but fortunately left intact one of its finest features — the long gallery in the North wing. Also intact is the charming gatehouse which was completed in 1658. Built of Cornish granite as is the rest of the house, the gatehouse with its niches, pillars and stumpy obelisks — repeated along the garden walls — reflects the growing Renaissance influence of the period. The rest of the house was rebuilt after the fire on the lines of the old and contains some original furniture and a collection of family portraits. It is open to the public from April to the end of October.

Mevagissey, Cornwall. Formerly a classic among Cornish fishing villages, Mevagissey has found tourists easier to catch than herrings. Nonetheless, from above or below it is a captivating spot. The inner harbour pier was built about 1770.

66

Fowey, Cornwall. Fowey — pronounced 'Foy' — is a miniature Dartmouth in more ways than one. Apart from its physical resemblance to the famous Devon harbour, it is one of the fountain heads of English naval greatness. The 'Gallants of Fowey' were constantly raiding the Normandy coast from the days of Edward III onwards, and the port has contributed its ships and sailors to the Royal fleets since the Siege of Calais. During World War II it was appropriately a base for motor torpedo boats operating in the Channel. Nowadays it is an attractive harbour for visiting yachtsmen and has found a new prosperity as the main port for the flourishing china-clay export trade. The church on the left is St Nicholas and dates from 1336. Immediately behind it is Place House, the seat of the Treffry family since the early 16th century. It owes its battlements, towers and turrets, however, to the Gothic revival of the early 19th century.

Polperro, Cornwall. Though many people feel it a matter for the utmost regret that Polperro did not have a staircase for a main street like Clovelly to keep the cars out, it remains the paragon of Cornish fishing villages. The little river Rafiel runs into the head of the harbour under a tiny stone bridge reputed to be Saxon in origin.

Looe, Cornwall. The towns of West and East Looe are built on either side of a deep wooded river valley and are joined together by the seven arch bridge seen here. Looe has a long history as a seaport — one quayside church dates back to the 12th century — and has served the multiplicity of roles of all Cornish ports over the centuries from fishing, smuggling and the export of silver and tin from mines on Bodmin moor through to its present one as a very popular holiday resort and a centre for sailing and shark fishing.

Denham Bridge, River Tavy, Devon. The River Tavy that gives its name to Tavistock rises high on Dartmoor on the slopes of the 1,900ft Amicombe Hill. On its long descent to the sea in the Tamar Estuary, it meanders through a succession of deep cut gorges and ravines like the one spanned here by Denham bridge which carries the road from Buckland Monachorum to Bere Alston. Quiet and gentle though they appear in dry weather these Dartmoor rivers quickly become raging torrents when the Atlantic storms break over the Moor.

74

Salcombe, Devon. Sheltered, safe, southerly — Salcombe harbour is particularly well blessed and has been likened to a Mediterranean resort in an English setting. The warm wet climate encourages the growth of exotic hedgerow flowers and shrubs like magnolias and fuchsias. Earlier in its history Salcombe was famous for shipbuilding and especially for its schooner-rigged Salcombe clippers used during the 19th century in the fruit trade from the Mediterranean. Sharpitor House overlooking the harbour mouth is owned by the National Trust and contains a splendid museum of ship models from those days.

River Dart near Dittisham Ferry, Devon. The River Dart rises in the heart of Dartmoor near Cranmere Pool and is 36 miles long. The ten miles from Totnes to Dartmouth are tidal — another of the drowned river valleys called 'rias' — and Dittisham is just over two miles upstream from Dartmouth in one of the most enchanting reaches of an outstandingly beautiful estuary. This area of the Dart has associations with Sir Walter Raleigh — he is said to have smoked the first pipefuls of new found tobacco on the Anchor Stone a few hundred yards downstream.

78

River Dart near Hexworthy, Dartmoor, Devon. The same river but closer to its source on Dartmoor near to Dartsmeet where the waters of the East Dart and the West Dart merge. The eastern slopes of Dartmoor tend to be softer, warmer and drier than the western and gentle fertile valleys like the one seen here are in sharp contrast with the bleak wildness of the high tors in whose shelter they lie.

80

Dartmoor, 'Black Hill', Widecombe, Devon. Not far from Widecombe in the Moor is 'Black Hill', one of the Dartmoor heights rising to 1,300ft. The grotesque twisted granite rocks shrouded in mist with the wind howling about them make an ideal setting for tales of mystery and imagination in which the region abounds. Not for nothing did Conan Doyle send Sherlock Holmes to Grimpsound, a prehistoric settlement not far away, to begin his hunt for *The Hound of the Baskervilles*.

82

Widecombe in the Moor, Devon. Widecombe is renowned for two things. First, for Widecombe Fair made famous by the song about 'Uncle Tom Cobleigh and all' and which is held on the second Tuesday in September. Second, for its church with its 120ft tower built 400 years ago by the tin miners thankful for the prosperity then prevailing. And, it is said, Uncle Tom Cobleigh's chair can still be seen in the church.

Dart Valley Railway, Devon. A Dart Valley Railway train approaching Riverford Bridge, near Staverton. This preserved steam railway, reopened in 1969, meanders along the banks of the river Dart from Buckfastleigh to Totnes. In this picture one of the railway's ex-GWR tank locomotives is hauling a train composed of the 'Devon Belle' observation car and other interesting rolling stock. Open to the public, it operates from Easter until September.

Totnes, Devon. A gateway within a gateway — East Gate once marked the eastern boundary of the medieval walled town of Totnes at the head of the navigable tidal estuary of the River Dart. Legend has it that Brutus the Trojan who gave his name to Britain and became its first king landed at Totnes. From him stemmed a host of famous British kings — from Lear and Cymbeline to Old King Cole and King Arthur, the once and future king. The Saxons used the port and so did the Normans who fortified it. Its busiest period was between the 14th and 17th centuries when it became prosperous from the export of wool and cloth. Its quay is still used for the import of timber but only at the cost of constant dredging. East Gate itself suffered from the Victorian restorers hence its Gothic battlements and cupola. At one time it had separate arches and gates for horse-drawn vehicles and foot traffic and was part of the old wall. It now serves to mark the change from steep and narrow Fore Street to the even steeper and narrower High Street.

88

Berry Pomeroy Castle, near Totnes, Devon. Often regarded as the most romantic ruin in Devon, Berry Pomeroy is the site of two castles built by two celebrated families. The de Pomerais were favourites of William the Conqueror and held the estate from 1066 until 1548. They built the first castle towards the end of the 13th century and only the ruined gatehouse, seen here, and the Lady Margaret Tower remain standing today. The gatehouse leads into a narrow courtyard which is the site of the second castle built but never completed in the 16th century by the Seymour family — the Duke of Somerset, the Protector of Edward VI and brother to Henry VIII's wife, Jane Seymour, bought the estate from the de Pomerais in 1548. The ruin of the 16th century castle with its mullioned windows can be seen here on the left of the photograph. The castle suffered severely during the Civil War and was falling down when William of Orange was entertained here in 1688 after he landed at nearby Brixham. William is said to have held his first Parliament in a thatched house in Longcombe, a mile from the castle.

Brixham, Devon. Brixham is a place that has seen much national history. Drake in his ship the *Golden Hind* — a replica of which is pictured here — brought his first Armada capture into Brixham. William of Orange landed here on Guy Fawkes' Day 1688, consummating the 'Glorious Revolution'. In August 1815 Napoleon, aboard the *Bellerophon*, spent a week off Brixham awaiting the sentence that was to send him to exile and eventual death in St Helena, after his 'revolution' had ended at Waterloo. And it was at Brixham that Henry Francis Lyte, then vicar of the parish church of All Saints, wrote the renowned English hymn *Abide with Me*. The statue of King William in the foreground was unveiled on the bicentenary of his landing at Brixham on 5 November 1888.

Thatcher Rock, Torquay, Devon. Around the Torbay area are several large outcrops of Devonian limestone, a carboniferous rock similar to that found in the Pennines in Derbyshire and the Yorkshire Dales and also on the French riviera. Limestone cliffs and bluffs, the mild climate, palm trees and clumps of pine running down to the edge of the cliff have earned this region the title of English Riviera. Thatcher Rock depicted here, a typical limestone formation, has tended to be undermined and eroded by the wetter elements in the atmosphere.

Oddicombe Beach, Babbacombe, Devon. An interesting contrast in rock formation — red sandstone cliffs running north to the mouth of the River Exe and on to Budleigh Salterton, a rugged outcrop of limestone that is Petit Tor point. Marble is found at Petit Tor and just south of Babbacombe is a celebrated limestone cave, Kent's Cavern. It is one of the oldest recognisable human dwelling places in the country and contains the remains of bears and other large animals sealed into the floor of the cave by stalagmite action.

Coryton Cove, Dawlish, Devon. Isambard Kingdom Brunel the Victorian genius of railway development built his main line to the west on the strand between Dawlish and the sea — such things could be done in those days — and threaded it through the red sandstone rocks. There are five tunnels in all and the entrances to two of them are visible here. Passengers on the railway have enjoyed their view of the sea and the strangely shaped rocks — the celebrated Parson and Clerk rocks are on the right — since December 1846. Since then they have also enjoyed a variety of forms of locomotion from Brunel's unsuccessful experiments with his 'Atmospheric Railway' through varieties of steam to present day HST.

Cathedral Close, Exeter. An intimate corner of Exeter's superb cathedral close — the approach to The Quadrangle now the Bishop of Crediton's house. (Crediton is a suffragan bishopric to the see of Exeter which was transferred to the security of the walled city in 1050.) The courtyard dates from about 1450 and the building may have been the Hostel of St John the Baptist of an even earlier date. Considerable alterations were made in the Jacobean period (1600-1630) and the elaborately studded and diamanted doors on the left date from that period. Notice the portal in the main door. Above the doorway of the house are the arms of Bishop Cotton who died in 1621.

Mol's Coffee House, Cathedral Close, Exeter. A gem of an Elizabethan house, 'Mol's Coffee House' has been carefully and lovingly restored and is one of the most perfect examples of Tudor architecture in this country. The oriel windows are a particularly attractive feature. The Dutch gable dates only from 1885.

Manor House, Hayes Barton, East Budleigh, Devon. Walter Raleigh, Devon's greatest son, was born here in 1552 and the house had undoubtedly been built a good deal earlier than that. It is made of cob and though its walls were at some time rendered with cement mortar over the traditional lime-wash, it is a remarkable testimony to the durability of that ancient method of building. It is thought to be the largest surviving cob building in the United Kingdom. The house is open to visitors in the summer.

Landscape near Pinn, Sidmouth, Devon. The early morning autumn sun lifts the pile of the stubble, wakes up the rooks out of the trees and glints through the mist on the well-filled silage hoppers at the farmstead. This is the mellow country face of Devon that on this halcyon day would be reflected in a myriad of valleys — gentle wooded hills, deep hedged lanes with stands of oak and beech, limewashed cob cottages and thatched roofs — all timeless and quite unforgettable.

106

Sidmouth, Devon. Sidmouth takes its name from the little River Sid which in earlier times provided a small but sheltered harbour. As has happened elsewhere along the English Channel coast, the sea has thrown up a shingle bank across the river mouth and closed it except at the top of spring tides. As is evident here, the few remaining fishing boats operate from the beach. The hill above them is Salcombe Hill — not to be confused with the other Salcombe further south and west — which marks a temporary end of the red sandstone coast. There is then a limestone outcrop which runs eastwards to Beer. Both Salcombe and Beer stone were once much used in building and Exeter Cathedral has large quantities of both.

Bicton Gardens, East Budleigh, Devon. Celebrated for its avenue of Chile pines — known in this country as monkey puzzles — Bicton gardens were laid out in 1735 to designs by Le Notre, the architect of the gardens at the palace of Versailles. The buildings with the Ionic columns and pediment is the orangery built in the early 19th century.

110

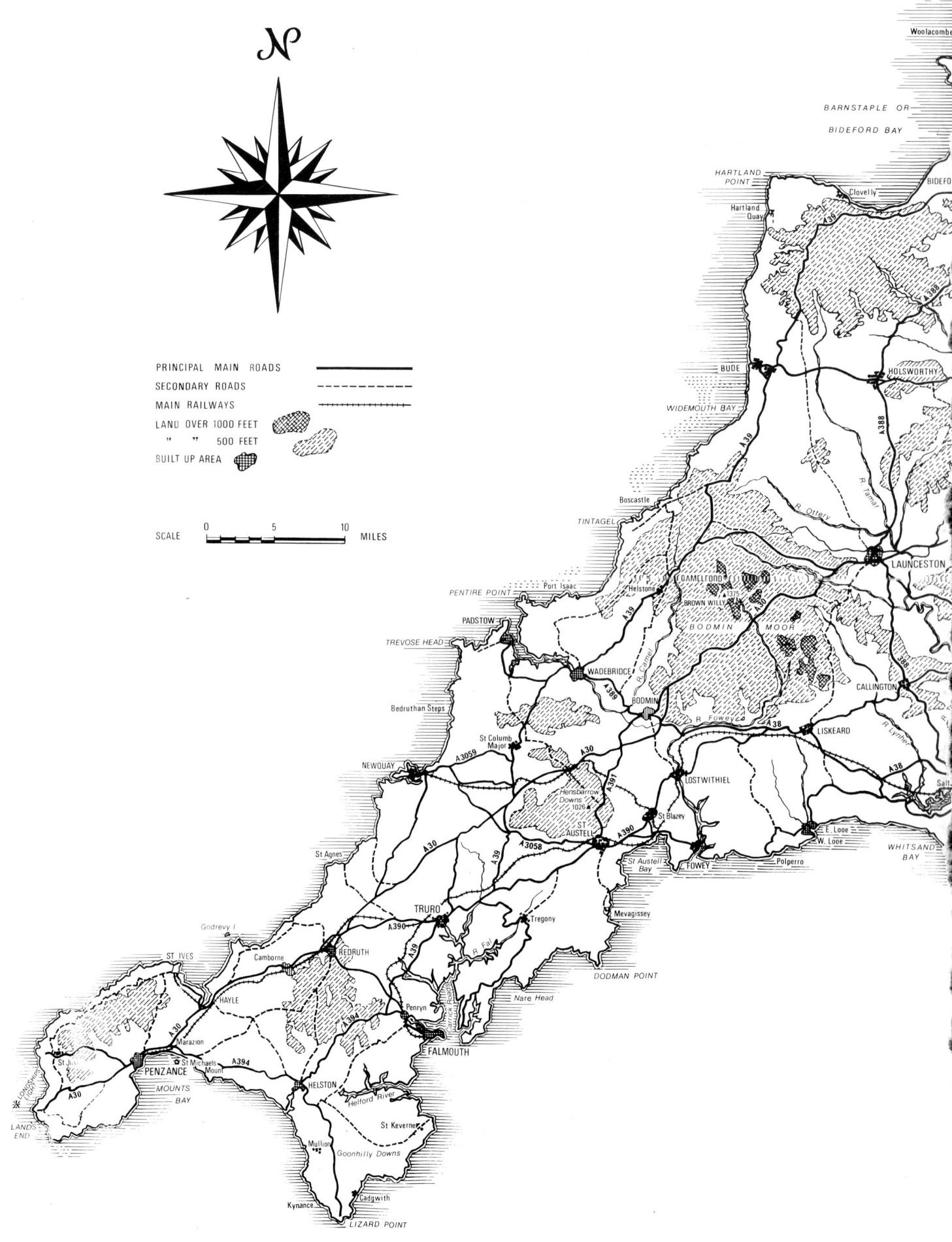

N

PRINCIPAL MAIN ROADS
SECONDARY ROADS
MAIN RAILWAYS
LAND OVER 1000 FEET
" " 500 FEET
BUILT UP AREA

SCALE 0 5 10 MILES

Woolacombe

BARNSTAPLE OR
BIDEFORD BAY

HARTLAND
POINT
Clovelly
BIDEFOR
Hartland
Quay

BUDE
HOLSWORTHY
WIDEMOUTH BAY

Boscastle

TINTAGEL
Port Isaac
PENTIRE POINT
PADSTOW
TREVOSE HEAD
CAMELFORD
Helstone
BROWN WILLY
BODMIN MOOR
LAUNCESTON

Bedruthan Steps
WADEBRIDGE
BODMIN
CALLINGTON
St Columb
Major
R Fowey
LISKEARD
NEWQUAY
A3059
A30
A391
LOSTWITHIEL
St Agnes
Hensbarrow
Downs
1026
A39
A3058
St Blazey
ST
AUSTELL
A390
E. Looe
W. Looe
WHITSAND
BAY
St Austell
Bay
FOWEY
Polperro
TRURO
A390
Tregony
Mevagissey
Godrevy I.
DODMAN POINT
ST IVES
Camborne
REDRUTH
R Fal
Nare Head
HAYLE
A39
Penryn
Carrick Roads
St Ives
Marazion
St Michaels
Mount
FALMOUTH
PENZANCE
A394
HELSTON
LANDS
END
MOUNTS
BAY
Helford River
St Keverne
Mullion
Goonhilly Downs
Kynance
Cadgwith
LIZARD POINT